Roots and Wings— Poems to My Daughter

*It is with some sadness
(The right of every loving parent),
But also with great pride
(The right of every loving parent),
That I watch you moving on to find
New mountains to climb,*
  New friends to meet, and
    A new life to begin.

Other Bestselling Books by Blue Mountain Press

Blue Mountain Press®

Boulder, Colorado

Roots and Wings— Poems to My Daughter

*Your Growing Up and
Moving Away from Home
Hasn't Been Easy for Me*

Roger A. Desmarais, Ph.D.

Dedication:

To Suzie, my wife,
who made me a father,
who trusted me to be a father,
who loved me in my fathering,
who is my better half
in her mothering.

Copyright © 1996 by Roger Desmarais.
Copyright © 1996 by Blue Mountain Arts, Inc.

Library of Congress Catalog Card Number: 95-26686
ISBN: 0-88396-423-6

⌐⌐ design on book cover is registered in U. S. Patent and Trademark Office.

Manufactured in the United States of America
First Printing: January, 1996

Library of Congress Cataloging-in-Publication Data

Desmarais, Roger A.
    Roots and wings : poems to my daughter : your growing up and
  moving away from home hasn't been easy for me / Roger A. Desmarais.
        p.   cm.
    ISBN 0-88396-423-6 (alk. paper)
    1. Fathers and daughters—Poetry.   I. Title.
PS3554.E839R66   1996
811'.54—dc20   95-26686
                                                            CIP

This book is printed on fine quality, laid embossed, 80 lb. paper. This paper has been specially produced to be acid free (neutral pH) and contains no groundwood or unbleached pulp. It conforms with all of the requirements of the American National Standards Institute, Inc., so as to ensure that this book will last and be enjoyed by future generations.

Blue Mountain Press ®

P.O. Box 4549, Boulder, Colorado 80306

CONTENTS

Daughter, Your Growing Up and Moving Away from Home Hasn't Been Easy for Me

It is with some sadness
(The right of every loving parent),
But also with great pride
(The right of every loving parent),
That I watch you moving on to find
New mountains to climb,
New friends to meet, and
A new life to begin.

Your moving away from home
Has changed my life focus.
I now find myself in a new role—
There is less need for me to fulfill
Obligations that were begun at your birth
And nurtured through the years.
I understand your need to make your own way—
To walk your own walk,
Talk your own talk,
And I love seeing you
Making strides on your own.
I marvel at your energy,
I love your enthusiasm,
I support your desire to go out
And experience the world
As deeply as possible.

Yet I still feel nervous
And lonesome sometimes;
I still want certain things for you.
Your voice continues to echo in your room
And down the hallway at home.
In the memories of my mind,
I still hear your voice and see your beauty.
I am proud of you, Daughter,
I love you very much,
And I can't help but miss you.

Thinking of You and Missing You, Daughter

*My mind continually wanders
   to thoughts of you —
Both present and future.
Your voice has a different quality now.
Your thoughts have a greater expanse.
Your experiences are impressive.
Your expectations have no boundaries,
   and I like that.*

*I am so pleased
With what you have done
And will continue to accomplish.
My prayers are that you will
Make wise decisions;
Choose your friends for both
Their personalities and their values;*

Work at being a significant person,
An extraordinary friend,
A person of courage,
Honesty,
And integrity,
And a young woman who understands
The beauty and value of being
A good human being
In any
And all
Situations.

Above all else,
Always remember that
I love you
Regardless of what you do,
Because you are a wonderful,
Caring, and loving person.

Roots and Wings—
The Greatest Gifts
We Can Give
to Our Children

A good friend once said that
The greatest gifts we can give
To our children are:

Roots —
A solid place from which to begin
Based on love, discipline,
Opportunities, support,
Encouragement to go the extra mile
And the resources to do so,
An environment of family and friends.

Wings —
The courage and motivation
To try one's flight,
To go where you've never been before,
To reach out and touch
A whole new world of the mind,
Feelings, insights, ideas, and friends...

This good friend also said,
"You will be happy when your children
Take the wind in their wings
And fly away to search the world."
However, that friend forgot to speak to the
Roots when the wings have flown.
Here, where the shelter of the beginning
Has become a transition to elsewhere,
The waiting begins—
The listening to what is said
And not said
In the letters and
Over the magical lines of long distance.
The distance is the thing that hurts.
But what would wings be without distance?
What would roots be without a place
From which wings have flown?

It is a paradox of the bittersweet
When fathers and mothers
Watch their handiwork move out,
Onward and upward,
Leaving roots behind.
No one can fill the void,
Except the one who has left.
But that is the sweet satisfaction of
Successful parenting,
And the pain of that success
Can only be felt in the giver.

Eventually,
Homesickness and loneliness
Will be replaced
With the joy and bounty
Of a new life.
But the void will remain a void,
Filled with memories and pictures
Of the good old days
When youth was experiencing roots
And parents basked in
The joy of providing them.

And yet,
As I look back across the years
And see the wonderful person
You have become—
Moving into your own,
Grabbing for the brass ring,
Stretching to the ultimate,
Trying on a new coat of life,
Tasting and touching the roses—
I am happy knowing that you are
Doing what you were meant to do.
You may have moved away, but
A part of you remains behind.

Is This the Little Girl?

I have a memory of you
As a little girl—
Singing your heart out
On the stage of my heart,
In the halls of my mind,
Viewed from the orchestra pit
Of our family room.

I have a memory of you
As a young woman—
During the last years of your childhood,
Before that stage of life when
Responsibility leads to accountability,
Yearning to be on with your life,
Displaying your courage and eagerness
To move on.

I have a memory of you
Looking back one last time—
About to turn away and walk into the
Future on your own,
Guided by whatever good
You have accepted from the past
And open to whatever good
Will be presented to you in the future...

I have a yearning —
To once more hold you close,
To once again be a significant force
In your young life,
To feel the fires of parental pride,
To produce another victory together
Against whatever childhood challenge we face,
To just once more be the
Young parent.

But that little girl is now gone —
Not gone — just removed, moved on,
Distanced through time and space,
Leaving behind old memories
And promising new,
Taking control of the ship,
Seeking out the uncharted waters,
Rising to the challenge of a new land —
A promised land —
A place called "mine."

I need to be a star in your sky:
To see the wake in your distance,
To be close to every change in your course —
Not to direct, but to support,
Not to persuade, but to approve,
Not to deny, but to be there
For whatever truth is to be shared,
For whatever insight might be valuable.

And so today,
I reflect on the passage of your life
In the video of my mind.
And I am pleased —
Pleased that you came from me,
Pleased that you can leave me,
Pleased that you will return to me
Your own woman,
My own daughter...
A joy
A pain
A tear
A promise
A love.

A father's little girl
Is a very precious package—
All dolled up in pink,
Ribbons in the hair,
Sash at the waist,
Shiny black dancing shoes
Flashing in the sunlight
Of summers past.

And then she grows up...

Ribbons in the hair still exist
With a twist to keep
The rich cascading tresses
From blowing in the wind;
Colors of the rainbow,
With special attention to
Complimentary shades,
Provide variety to original pink;
Shoes made for walking
Now move you along the road
Into the future.

Yes, a father's little girl
Is still a precious package—
All dolled up in grown-up clothes,
Carrying books of wisdom
From room to class and back,
Meeting her world peers,
Reaching out,
Touching others,
Growing into a more wonderful
Person than before.
The wonder of it all.
It couldn't be otherwise.

First Steps

Watching you grow
Has been a joy to me.
The baby years were special:
First words, first steps,
First everything.
Grade-school years were special:
First grades, first experiences,
Socialization of the independent spirit,
Education of the mind
In a formal setting.
High-school years were special:
First competitive successes blended with
First academic accomplishments of worth.
And now,
College years are so very special:
A visit to your campus gives us
An opportunity to walk around,
To meet your friends,
To spend quiet time together
Discussing life, yours and mine,
And the goals of a beautiful young lady
Who is so far removed from
Those first steps
Yet who is again taking first steps,
This time into the world.

Stimulated by recent experiences
Of success and accomplishment,
You are eager to get on with your vision,
To impact the world,
Do something of merit,
And you are impatient with the process
Of preparation for
Those other first steps
Into the future
Yet to come.

I am overjoyed
With the feelings of pride
In who you are,
What you have accomplished,
What you want to be.
You, my daughter, will take
Many more first steps into life.
That is what discovery of life
Is all about.
And though you don't need
My hand as you used to,
It is nice of you
To ask for my advice
Once in a while
When first steps are scary.
It is nice when a parent
Can still be a parent
Once in a while.

A Parent's Needs

Deep within a parent's heart
Beats a need to make the world good.
There is hope that "the kids" will grow
To be strong and healthy
With good values and ideas,
Healthy habits and minds.

Deeper within that heart beats a need
For the kids to love one another,
To know that blood is thicker than water,
That family is the bastion of
Hope and support, love and care.
There is a need to have the kids mesh
With the heartbeat of the father's needs,
And the mother's,
For when that happens,
All the other pains go away.

To be able to look on the family at play,
In discussion, at the dinner table,
Going out the door, coming in the door,
Laughing and touching...
That's what makes the world better
And justifies all the trying.
It is the reward for parents
Loving their kids — to the end.
The vision of the children
Enjoying their time together —
That is what it is all about.

Thanks for the vision;
Thanks for the reward;
Thanks for the love.

$\mathcal{A}$ Time of Transition

Without doubt, growth is pain.
Inwardly, your desire for separation
Demands distance from
What once was comfortable,
Trusted, rewarding, and life giving.
There is a need to be "out there"
Establishing one's self
As someone worthy of standing
On one's own feet.

That need for separation is as strong
As the wild bird's migration north and south,
The flow of rivers down the course of gravity,
The snow in winter,
Rose blossoms in the spring.
Inwardly, that call of the wild
Must be answered or one will perish
In what was comfortable.

I remember past migrations of my own soul—
Rising to meet the challenge,
Struggling to solve the mysteries of life,
Experiencing new relationships,
Fearing whatever the worst might be,
Marching to my own drumbeat.
Now, standing by and watching
The changes in you taking place,
I can only be proud.

Yes, it seems as though the time has come—
Or is coming still—
When you will move.
Initial talk about the old chair,
A bookshelf here, an iron there—
It is beginning to form a pattern
That eventually will lead to separation.

And so, I sit here trying to capture
In fragile vessels of words
The deep-down feelings in my heart
And cannot do justice to the thoughts
And feelings that well up,
Except to say that migrations have been
Part of evolution for all times past
And all times to come.
We live with what we must become
And become better for it.

So fly, my daughter,
On your wonderful wings of
Courage and insight,
Trust and love,
Intelligence and wisdom,
Brightness and beauty.
Continue to grow and develop,
And remember your roots
From the old days
As you look forward
With your wings.

This Is a New Beginning for Both of Us

Another milestone,
Though it feels more like a millstone,
Weighs down my spirit,
Measures the length of my heart,
Tests the strength of my belief,
Shapes the future
Of our relationship.
Another milestone—
A new beginning for you,
A new ending for me.

I try to discern
The inner workings of my spirit
As I try to visualize
The workings of your spirit
As you plan and plot
In this summer of your life
To live away from home
Alone
With other friends
In a new place.

I try to anticipate
Your room without your song,
Evenings without your laughter,
Family discussions without your philosophy,
Late-night talks without your reflections,
Days and nights
Without you.

I try to visualize
Your new apartment
Sparse with early beginnings,
Your mornings of franticness,
Your evenings of tiredness,
Your midnight moods
Reflecting on your
Days and nights
Of new beginnings
In a world you are determined
To conquer.

I actually don't have a problem
Visualizing your new life;
I can see you
Taking the world
By storm
With your smile,
With your energy,
With your intelligence,
With your love.

What I can't quite anticipate
Is my first summer
Of my first loss
Without you
Here
At home.

The Airport Thing

Much of my life is spent
Moving into or out of
Airports
Watching people
Cry in sadness
At losing someone,
Cry in happiness
At receiving someone.
I marvel at the
Objectivity of those who
Stand and watch
Untouched by the meeting
And leave-taking.

And so,
The other morning,
As I watched you, my darling daughter,
Gradually moving towards the gate,
Passing on your ticket,
Passport to another town
Across time zones,
I wondered why no one understood
The tears in my eyes
And the catch in my voice
And the sadness in my heart
And the joy in my life
As I watched my daughter
Move on to take her
Place with the rest
Who are out to change the world.

There is a pride that overcomes,
That no one can imagine
Unless having felt it firsthand—
A pride in a person
Who is a mix of two people
Who in love created another
And fell in love with all the
Quirks and peculiarities,
Charm and beauty,
Of this child
Who carries on the genes
And the parts of us
That we consider the best.

There is a pride that only
Pain can bring
As tears fall from eyes
That no longer can see.
But you will return,
And my ears once again
Will be filled with sounds
Of laughter and old familiar
Words that profile the beauty
Of you, my darling daughter.
My heart will be filled with happiness
On that day
When the airport
Is again a place of gladness
And the tears at the gate
Turn into the joy of the return
Of one who has left,
But not left—
One who remains my dear,
Wonderful, darling daughter.

Long-Distance Dad

Looking at distance
Proves very difficult for me.
I seem to be nearsighted!
It is hard to focus on
The real issues of separation
Between a dad and his daughter.
Stories in the local paper
Speaking of rape in a van
And a young man lying in a coma
Because he drank too much
And fell four stories
Fuel my fear, and I wonder:
How involved do you get in parties?
How hard is the peer pressure?

Stop, I say to myself.

It is just hard to let go.
There is a void in my heart,
And I can't see.
It is the one who moves on
Who has all the vision,
Because that is what moving on
Is all about.
I remember that,
Yet it doesn't make it easier.
It is hard not to be able
To pass on wisdom
Gathered through the years,
Which now can only be hinted at,
Pointed to,
And discussed theoretically.
The process of learning,
Of becoming wise,
Is the same for you
As it was for me.
You are on your own now
With gentle nudges from me.
And I am still gaining wisdom, too,
Which I probably will find hard
Not to share with you.
So, I will tell you,
And you will listen,
And then you will do
Whatever you need to do.

Well, How Is She?

When you left home,
You left holes in people's hearts,
People who remember you
For who you are,
A valuable person who is missed.

Now people in the strangest places
Recognize me,
Not for who I am
But because of who you are to them.
I used to react to a smile or wave
From someone I really didn't know
Or couldn't remember,
Thinking they remembered me.
Now, however, I have learned
That they merely see in me
A messenger from you,
To fill their questions about
"How is she doing?"

And so I embellish the facts,
Speaking of how you relish the new.
Reports of your happiness
Delight the hearers
And stoke the embers of my pride,
So that I walk away
With high steps.
I am so happy in the knowledge
That whatever sacrifices
Are made at this end
Are worth it at your end;
Whatever concerns and anxieties
Might quiver in my heart
Register hope and joy,
Openness and drive,
In your heart.

I hope you will continue with your spirit up
And your eyes forward.
You are beginning the steps to being on your own.
Your decisions count now, more than ever.
You will live with the consequences and results
As your own—uncontaminated or diluted
By direct input from me.
And I have no fear of your decisions.
You have what I tried to pass on
And have made that your own.
Be wise beyond your years
And see with more than your eyes,
Hear with more than your ears,
And step into the future with courage.
You are on the right track.

The Face in the Pumpkin

Another first.
Feeling the frost in the morning air,
Noticing the leaves turn from green to brown
And signs on the roadways that say:
PUMPKIN PATCH—SELECT YOUR OWN.
I remember when you could barely crawl
Over the high mounds of orange fruit
Slipping to the side,
Laughing with joy,
Wondering what it was all about,
This buying of crazy orange balloons full of goo.

The years seemed to flow
Like a slide show of still images:
Carving pumpkins on various kitchen tables,
Hoping not to cut off a finger,
Trying to be "oh, so creative"
With textured pumpkin skin.
Mine were always straight lines
And triangle noses;
Yours were rounded and indented and wonderful.
Years of metal trays full of pumpkin seeds,
Roasted, but rarely eaten.

This year, we do it without you,
But I'll buy a special one and put it aside
And visualize your hands
And your face
And your heart.

Your Room Is Quiet Now

Your old room
Experiences silence now—
An emptiness filled
With memories of days gone by,
Of laughter and tears,
Late-night phone calls,
And early morning struggles
To face another day—
Noises of the good old days.

Now your bed is made—
Day and night!
The floor is clear and neat,
Books are all in a row,
Awards hang on the wall
Beside pictures of special moments
And friends.

Nightly,
A quick flick of my wrist
On the light switch
Captures the emptiness.
There in the soft light
I whisper a silent good-night
And listen quietly
To the sounds of the past
That are held in the paper and wood
Demanding to be heard again.

And so, your empty bedroom
Speaks to me daily
Of a time gone by.
But also of a current
Place and time
And of another room that
Now holds your spirit,
Is warmed by your humor and laughter,
And charmed by your words and sounds.

Two-Edged Sword

Our telephone conversation was heavy—
Weighed down with discussions
Of new realities,
Of friendships being tested,
Relationships bent under pressure,
Decision-making tension.
There was the wistful, unspoken wish
That things could be simpler,
As in days long gone,
Days at home when school was
Merely school.

Then there was a moment of silence;
A bit of input from another voice
Interrupts our conversation,
And you go away to another line
To connect with another world...

When you come back,
There is a blast of joy,
A cry of wonderment,
A sudden change in velocity
Greeting my resting ear
As you convey to me
That somebody out there,
Somebody who held your future
In their hands,
Actually wants you,
Would love to have you,
Work in their company for the summer.

And so we dance our happy dance
Through the phone
As you eloquently explain
The virtues of said company —
The beauty of the building,
The friendliness of the employees,
The ambiance of its workplace,
And your excitement is contagious.
My heart jumps with joy inside,
For you, my daughter,
Have triumphed
In the big world
Of the marketplace.

Gone is the sadness from before;
Gone is the melancholy
And heaviness of trying to be wise
In a world where imperfection
And perfection struggle to maintain
A precarious balance and
Symmetry of the soul.

You are alive and happy.
You have a job,
And it is wonderful.
However, after we hang up,
I reflect on how
That other phone call
Has sealed my fate
For this coming summer.
Your job is not nearby,
So you will be living away from home.
It is a two-edged sword.
However, right now I need to reflect
Only on the one edge;
I need to focus on your joy,
Which is easy to do.
I am thrilled with
The wise decision made
By some other person
Who doesn't know you
Or love you
Or care for you
As I do,
Yet who will have you
For the summer.

And so,
My happiness for your joy
Remains as true as
Its first pristine fervor.

If Only They Had Asked Me

I absolutely love hearing about
Your latest insights,
Hopes, and breakthroughs.
There are new dragons for you to slay—
Those of the marketplace.
And I revel in the thought
Of you out making your mark
On the world—
Proving that youth is wonderful,
Full of integrity and insight,
Ready to make a move
And stand the test
We all must face.
Someday, they may speak of you
In the marketplace,
Of your conquests and achievements.
They will tell those who follow you
That they, too, can be like you
If they have courage, intellect,
And insight.

I, however, could have
Told them that a long time ago.
I would have said:
Do not mess with the best there is.
Hire her!
Or forever rue the day
Your competition saw the light
And passed the torch
To this young woman of
Substance and integrity,
Hope and courage,
Love of life,
And eagerness to achieve.
No underachiever is she —
Only vision and mission,
Heart and soul,
Mind and spirit —
Ready to do battle
With the dragons of the marketplace.

Reconnecting

Rethinking the feeling
Of the past two weeks
You spent at home with us,
I feel sad.
The time slipped by too quickly.
There seemed to be a distance
In your eyes—
Perhaps exhaustion from
The late-night studying
To succeed at exams?
Perhaps something of a different nature?
Camouflaging questions of growth,
Independence, future, present, past?
Or were those questions
About where we were?
Where I was?

My belief in you is unwavering.
I burst at your presence,
Your accomplishments,
Your quests.
I struggle with your struggles.
I cry with your tears.
I laugh in your joy,
And I stand ready to do battle
With any and all
Of your vague or concrete demons.
However, I notice that
I stand more to the side these days—
Still ready, still poised,
But obliquely in the line of sight.
My role is more diminished these days.
Perhaps what I saw in your eyes
Was a reflection of mine
Asking how we reconnect;
At what level can you and I,
Daughter and father,
Let go of our more adolescent roles
In order to form a more
Adult "you and me"?

Voice on a Wire

There is something
So sweet,
So filled with energy,
So lovely,
About her voice
Coming to me from afar.
Enthusiasm and happiness
Coming to me on a wire—
Thin and stretched across
Half a continent,
Squeezedintomicrosecondsofelectricalbursts.
I want to
E l o n g a t e   t h e   w o r d s ,
Fill the quiet moments of time
With her presence,
Reach out and touch her.

How hard I listen to the variances,
The differences, in her voice—
The trembling at the edges,
The tear in the sound.
I wait beyond the words
For the truth to come.
I listen beneath the sounds
For the feeling of presence.
I try to decipher
The meaning behind the sound.

My world catches fire
When I hear her voice
On the wire.

You're Coming Home

The countdown has begun in earnest,
Because soon you will burst upon us.
Your room has never looked cleaner
And I cannot wait
To see it cluttered again
With old tennis shoes
Begging for retirement,
Piles of clothes
Waiting for the laundry,
Clusters of letters
Of untold imaginings,
And stacks of CDs
Ready to fill the house
With long-awaited new sounds.

However, since you've been gone,
Changes have taken place.
I have seen them
In your letters,
In your conversations,
In your visits,
In your insights about yourself,
In your demeanor towards others,
In your attitude towards life,
In your reaction to responsibilities,
In the texture of your love,
In the depth of your spirit,
In the quality of your heart.

You will come home a different person
Than when you left.
I look forward to the times
We will talk and laugh,
Listen and be silent,
Share the intricacies of our lives
Along with the silly topics.
I relish our past history together,
Walking down the path of life
To this moment.
Now I hold my breath—
Waiting for your return,
Waiting to cherish
The "from here on out,"
The new beginning
From an old past,
Both of which are wonderful—
Only now a bit changed
Because you grew up
And now bring home
A new beauty I hope to savor,
A new depth I hope to discern,
A new height I hope to contemplate,
A new wisdom I hope to appreciate.

Twenty-First Birthday

My deep-down feelings
Have been jangled lately;
My innermost thoughts
Have been jumbled,
As I contemplate the celebration
Of a very significant event:
Your twenty-first birthday,
My twenty-first birthday as your father.

There is no specific preparation
For such an event.
It just happens,
Though you prepared me
In your own inimitable way
By being yourself—
Independent and gracious,
Loving and determined,
Intelligent and practical,
Gentle and forgiving,
Sensitive and driven,
Motivated and successful.
As you prepared yourself
For moving on,
You also prepared me
For these years of
Leave-taking and coming back
As your own person,
In your own way...

My inside videotape
Replays those moments
When you first took breath
And smiled at me.
I hear your first sounds
Demanding attention and
Directing traffic from your crib.
I count the sidewalks of your life
When your little feet staggered
Hither and yon, ponytail bouncing,
Prancing along on tippee-toes.

I remember those magic moments
Of staggering insights
As you crossed the various thresholds
Of little girl to bigger girl;
Of young lady to a person of such wonder;
Through the years of
Educational development,
Emotional emancipation,
Spiritual insight, physical growth,
And psychological expansion;
Into womanhood
And all its mystery.

Your school years prepared me
For this moment at the end of college
When commencement really means
Beginning from where we left off.
I reflect on your studies,
Your achievements and successes,
Your promises for the future,
And I think, yes, the time has come.
I must let go a little more
And watch with pride
As you move on into the world
Of the future.

Yes, I think,
You have prepared me well
For this time when
I must move on from where I am
Without you.
Your courage and anxiety
About the future
Bolster my spirits and give me hope.

And so, I stand strong before the day
Of your twenty-first birthday
And take a deep breath
As you take another milestone step
Along the path to the future,
Away from roots
With wings to soar.

I look back at the day
Twenty-one years ago,
And I remember your smiles
Through the years,
Your laughter,
Your accomplishments,
And I know you are ready.
You are prepared.
And I want to let you go—
To wherever it is you will go—
With my support and love.

And I do.

Though, really,
I am not prepared.

Reflections on the Time Since You've Been Gone

It has been a very good year,
A time of joyous pride
In a job well done —
Not mine, not ours, not theirs —
But yours.

You moved on to begin a new life,
And it was clear
The last time you were here
That your mind had expanded,
Your emotions had matured,
Your insight into yourself
Had grown stronger,
Your world had enlarged.

But there was a void in your heart
When you were here with us,
A natural void —
To be filled with friends
From another place and time,
Experiences strange to the old home address,
Relationships changed through the growth of time,
Needs satisfied in different ways
Than before your leaving.

I watch the metamorphosis of change
With both sadness and pride
Because my girl is making her way,
Striding out,
Trying those wings fashioned in
The growing-up years.

Things were different this last time.
Your visit was quiet and gentle,
Filled with silent savoring
Of the old and familiar.
I see you marching to your own drummer now,
Singing to your own words,
Creating a song of your life
According to a much larger scale of notes
And range of control.
And I love it all.
I think you are marvelous—
Even when you are concerned
About love and life,
Grades and studies,
Friends and possibilities...

I look forward to the years to come.
I see you leading the way
With your spirit and enthusiasm,
Your charisma and enjoyment
Of friends and family and life.
I may have given you life many years ago.
I may have been around to provide
Guidance at times, direction at others,
And freedom in between.
I may have been slow to let go
And deluded into thinking that
Your growing-up years could have been
Managed more effectively.
But as you have grown into the lovely
Young woman that you have become,
You have taken those strides on your own,
With your own counsel and regard
For the consequences,
Your own application of virtue
In the context of a search
For the right and best way to live.
You have been and continue to be responsible
For your own future.

And so,
While I realize that you are being
Pulled out into another world of
Personal development
And distance from the past,
I also believe that there will always be
A connection between us and a return
To your roots in some form or another.
Parents freely and grudgingly
Give their children to the world.
Maybe that's the way we individually
Have to go out into the world:
Freely and excitedly — with a
Bit of anxiety and a yearning
For the comfort of the nest.

However, my dear daughter,
I do not grudgingly give you up
To the gravity of self-actualization,
Personal development, and individual insight.
I lovingly look forward to the future
And to the excitement
That you will bring into my life.
I am so proud of you and who you are
That sometimes I think my heart will break
With pride,
With love,
With delight
For you.

Ready, Set, Go!

I know you are prepared
For wherever the future takes you.
You have the tools and preparation,
The experience of hard work,
Of having to make it.
Yet, you also have experiences
Of taking the shortcut,
Of letting things ride without too much work.
Both knowledges —
One of dedication, one of procrastination —
Are with you today.
You must choose which one
You want to implement.

You are on your way —
Your way to succeed,
And I see you standing tall
In it all,
Aware of possibilities,
Potentials,
Opportunities for the future.
So take the challenge
And run with it.
But take care of yourself
Spiritually, physically,
Emotionally, and psychologically.
You will be stretched and prodded.
You will be tested and tempted.

It is all up to you,
My darling daughter,
As you move on into the future.

Never, Ever, Give Up on Your Dreams, and Remember... I Love You

My thoughts lately have been
On you—
Marveling as I do at
The promise of your life,
Your impact on the world,
Your sparkling sense of self.

You bring life to everything.
You have a smile that won't go away
And an energy that is unrivaled.
I see you making your mark on the world—
Your world, however large
You want it to be.
I see you breathing freshness
Into everything you do,
Creating light where
There had been murkiness,
Bringing awareness to your work
That is noticed and rewarded
With smiles of recognition
And friendship.
You have the right mixture
Of so many talents,
With a bit of shyness and nervousness,
Anxiety about doing things right,
And fear of doing them wrong.

I wish you could see yourself
The way I see you.
I wish you could appreciate —
And maybe you are beginning to —
The depth of who and what you are.
You are so vibrant and upbeat
In your general approach to life
That it is impossible for me not
To believe in you and your dreams.
You want to do your best at everything,
And then be even better than that.

Even apart from my built-in paternal bias,
I recognize in you a magical spirit
And the wisdom, truth,
And willingness to work hard
That makes you a winner.
Never doubt yourself,
And only criticize yourself
In order to get better.
Never, ever, give up on your dreams.
And remember that you have my
Unconditional support
And love.

Roots and Wings

Out of all the words of wisdom
About being a parent
That have been passed on to me,
One phrase, "Roots and Wings,"
Stands out.

Parents love to think of
Providing the foundation
Upon which a life can be built.
"Roots" are a place
From which and to which
One can travel in the mind.

However, "Wings," though they may
Sound soft and wonderful,
In reality, are harder to fathom,
Because wings fly away
And take from us those
For whom
Roots were made.

The important thing
To realize is that
Although wings take away,
They also bring back.

Wings fly both ways.

About the Author

To say that Roger Desmarais has led an interesting and varied life is definitely an understatement. Born in Washington State, Roger passed up a scholarship in 1953 to the University of Washington so he could join the Jesuit Religious Order. He has master's degrees in literature, education, theology, and philosophy, and was responsible for designing and directing Seattle University's prestigious Master of Religious Education program.

In 1971, Roger left the Jesuits and designed his own doctoral program in Organization Development and Human Relations. He married Suzie, his wife, in 1972 and began an impressive professional career that includes: Director of Training for VISTA in Kansas City, Director of Staff Development for Kaiser Permanente Hospitals in San Francisco, and Creator/Manager of Bechtel Power Corporation's Organization and Management Development Department in Los Angeles. In 1975, he founded his own management consulting practice. His firm was involved with the cleanup of Three Mile Island, resolving congressional concerns about the Alyeska Pipeline, and working with the Department of Energy on a number of significant projects.

Roger and Suzie like to spend as much time as possible with their three children: son, Michael, and daughters, Michelle and Jill, for whom this book was written. Roger has served on the boards of his children's schools and their communities, and even served as the local Commissioner of Little League Baseball for five years. In the future, he hopes to write management and leadership books based on experiences and insights he has developed through his consulting business.